Contents  KU-092-544

Introduction

Two Scotsmen, two Welshmen, two Ulstermen and two Englishmen are marooned on a desert island. The two Scotsmen get together and start a bank. The two Welshmen get together and start a choir. The two Ulstermen get together and start a fight. The two Englishmen never exchange a word as they haven't been formally introduced.

'British' is often used as a synonym for 'English'. England is by far the largest country in the United Kingdom, accounting for 54.7m people and 84% of the total population: Scotland has 5.3m (8%), Wales 3.1m (5%) and Northern Ireland 1.8m (3%). More than half of all English people see themselves as British first and foremost, as opposed to fewer than a third of Welsh people and fewer than a fifth of Scots.

There are times during *Haynes Explains The British* when, strictly speaking, it's the English rather than the British who are under discussion. But we did want to sell some copies north of Berwick, west of the Severn (see *Safety First!*) and indeed across the Irish Sea as well, so please bear with us. Besides, the bits in question are mainly the English-as-repressed-passive/aggressive-complainers bits, so frankly you're better off out of it, Jock, Taffy and Mick.

About this manual

The aim of this manual is to help you get the best value from the British. It can do this in several ways. It can help you (a) decide what work must be done (b) tackle this work yourself, though if you are a large corporation, you may choose to have much of it performed by external contractors such as a call centre in India, a small army of workers on zero-hour contracts and offices in Grand Cayman emphatically not placed there for tax purposes, oh no, indeed especially not if it's HMRC who's asking.

Tasks are described in a logical order so that even a novice can do the work. Although the specific requirements of the British can vary slightly according to age, class and region, fundamentally they all want variations on the following: somewhere serving 61 different varieties of beer, a kebab shop open till 5am, a kettle with cups, sugar, milk and teabags nearby, and an incompetent government to grumble about.

HAYNES EXPLAINS
THE BRITISH

Owners' Workshop Manual

© Haynes Publishing • Written by **Boris Starling**

Published in October 2017

A catalogue record for this book is available from the British Library

ISBN 978 1 78521 150 8

Haynes Publishing, Sparkford, Yeovil,
Somerset BA22 7JJ, UK
Tel: +44 (0) 1963 440635
Website: www.haynes.com

Haynes North America, Inc.,
861 Lawrence Drive, Newbury Park,
California 91320, USA

Printed and bound in Malaysia

Cover image from Getty Images

Illustrations taken from the
Haynes Austin Maestro
Owners Workshop Manual

Written by **Boris Starling**
Edited by **Louise McIntyre**
Designed by **Richard Parsons**

526 596 05 0

Safety first!

If you value your life, your livelihood, your liberty, your health, your home, your spouse, your children, your car, your pets, your possessions, your past, your present and your future – if you value any or all of those, never, never, never call anyone from Scotland or Wales 'English'. North of Berwick and west of the Severn, there is no greater insult. Don't believe it? Go to Murrayfield or the Millennium Stadium during the Six Nations and see what the locals think of England.

Working facilities

British working facilities vary greatly according to occupation. A courier is expected to deliver 82,347 parcels in 20 minutes across an area of 7,482 square miles. He will be hindered in this by the efforts of a workman who will have cordoned off 3,431 miles of road before going for a teabreak in order to meet the budget of a local government official who spends 98.65% of his work time in pointless meetings and 1.35% online ordering parcels to be delivered by a courier who....

Dimensions, weights and capacities

Overall height

Men .... 5'9". And no, we're not converting that into
.... centimetres for you, you namby-pamby
.... continentals. Work it out for yourself.
Women .... 5'3". 6'3" when wearing heels suitable either
.... for City board meetings or Newcastle nightclubs
.... on Friday night.
Ben Nevis................................... 4411'. Ben Ainslie: 6'. Ben Kingsley: 5'8".

Overall weight

Average man .... 13 stone. That's what he tells the doctor, anyway.
Average woman .... 11 stone. Has permanent option of shifting
.... unsightly lard by getting rid of husband.

Consumption

Beer.. Southerners: ½ pint per week.
.... Northerners: 10 pints per night (except Fridays
.... and Saturdays: 20 pints per night).
Tea.. 5 cups per hour, 24/7.

Engine

Stroke .... more and more likely if rising cholesterol levels
.... are anything to go by.
Power.. taking it (and control) back from Brussels by 2019.
Torque... Panellists on *Question Time*, endlessly.
Bore.. Harold in the corner of The Bugle who has a
.... conspiracy theory about everything – yes,
.... Harold, of course the Royal Family are
.... shape-shifting lizards.
Redline.. at the abject performance of any of our national
.... sports teams.

Interior

Cecil Rhodes said that 'to be born English is to win first prize in the lottery of life', and most English people would agree (as would most Scots, Welsh and Northern Irish if you substituted their nations for 'English'.) The British see themselves as amusing, decent, fair, polite and tolerant. They root for the underdog and like to take people down a peg or two when they've become too big for their boots. They like laws, and they like rules (especially unwritten ones): at the battle of Trafalgar, Admiral Collingwood refused to place snipers in the rigging because that wasn't the way proper chaps won naval battles.

An island race

The British are an island race, and it shows in their psyche. They regard their homes as their castles and consider themselves self-contained and self-sufficient. They don't go in for overt displays of patriotism – no saluting the flag, no pledges of allegiance – but give them a special occasion such as a royal jubilee and you could circle the earth with the amount of Union Jack bunting which comes out. There are many things you could put into a 'what it means to be British' list, but one of the most British things of all is the horror of even thinking about making such a list.

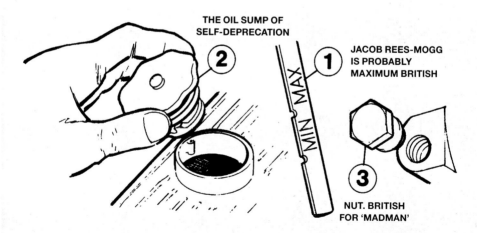

THE OIL SUMP OF
SELF-DEPRECATION

JACOB REES-MOGG
IS PROBABLY
MAXIMUM BRITISH

NUT. BRITISH
FOR 'MADMAN'

FIG 9•1 **CHECKING YOUR LEVELS: MAKING SURE YOU'RE TOPPED UP WITH BRITISHNESS**

⚠ Characteristics

The British define themselves and each other by region. Southerners think Northerners are backward and stupid: Northerners think Southerners are pretentious gits who can't hold their drink. West Country folk are thought of as cider-drinking carrot-crunching shitehawks. Scousers are scallies who'll have the hubcaps off your car before you can say 'Vauxhall Calibra'. And so on.

And that's just the English. The Scots refer to the English as the 'auld enemy' and consider England as what Scotland would be like without the mountains, glens, lochs and friendliness. (During the 1998 World Cup, when English fans were smashing up Marseilles and St. Etienne with gay abandon, only two Scottish fans were arrested all tournament – for fighting with a Frenchman who had refused to have a drink with them.)

The Welsh are big into rugby, music and sheep, not necessarily (a) in that order (b) literally. Famous Welsh rugby players include J.P.R. Williams, J.J. Williams, Martyn Williams, Shane Williams, Mervyn Davies, Gerald Davies, Jonathan Davies and Gareth Davies. Famous Welsh songs include 'Guide Me O Thou Great Redeemer,' 'Delilah' and, especially for the English holidaymakers, 'Summertime And Your

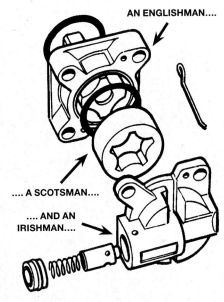

AN ENGLISHMAN....

.... A SCOTSMAN....

.... AND AN IRISHMAN....

FIG 9·2 **.... TRY TO ASSEMBLE AN ENGINE. THEN GIVE UP AND WALK INTO A PUB**

Houses Are Burning'. Famous Welsh sheep are too numerous to mention.

The Northern Irish are best known around the world for The Troubles, which involved three decades of conflict, the presence of the British army, marches by men dressed in bowler hats which made them look like Mr Benn, enormous murals on every spare piece of wall, and a few U2 songs.

Exterior

How the British see the French

The British (a) love the French (b) hate the French (c) hate themselves for loving the French (d) love themselves for hating the French. Few things confuse the British more than the French.

They love French culture, food, wine, fashion and climate. They hate French snobbery, superiority, pretentiousness and excitability. They think (with good reason) that British music is about a million times better than French music.

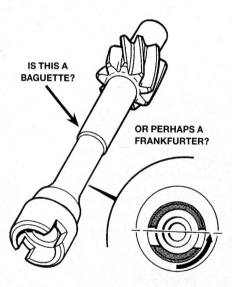

IS THIS A BAGUETTE?

OR PERHAPS A FRANKFURTER?

FIG 9•3 **CRANKING UP THE SUSPICION: THE BRITISH VIEW OF EUROPEANS**

They're jealous of the French's reputation as lovers extraordinaires and aren't sure how to deal with their free and frank attitudes towards sex. They cite almost 1,000 years of conflict from William the Conqueror all the way to Napoleon and beyond. They find the French attitudes towards personal hygiene disturbing and their refusal to speak English disconcerting. Ask a Briton to think of the French and write down random words which come to mind, and among them will be 'subsidies', 'Agincourt', 'corruption', 'blockades' and 'Sacha Distel'.

Basically, the British think the French would be greatly improved by being more British.

How the British see the Germans

The British aren't much like the French and hate it. The British are very much like the Germans and hate it.

Look what the British and the Germans have in common. They're both northern European nations with dodgy weather. They're both sticklers for rules and regulations. They're both much more uptight than their southern and Latin neighbours. They both like to drink beer. They both have a dry sense of humour and an advanced sense of manners. They both like dogs. The last time a French monarch was on the British throne was in 1399: the last time a German monarch was on the British throne was, er, now.

Ask a Briton to think of the Germans and write down random words which come to mind, and among them will be 'sunloungers', 'lederhosen', 'unsmiling', 'mullet' and 'Jurgen Klinsmann'.

Basically, the British think the Germans would be greatly improved by being more British, until it's pointed out that they already are.

How the British see the Americans

The British don't really know what to make of the Americans.

On one hand, there's the 'special relationship' and all that goes with it, such as the bonding of a common language and the historical ties of military and political alliances. The British love American films and music. They admire the Americans' optimism and can-do attitude. They think New York is the coolest city on earth. They love the fact that Americans love their accents.

On the other, there are the things about Americans that the British just don't understand. Guns, for a start. The emphasis on college sports and how college football teams can pack out 120,000-seat stadia. Sports only the Americans play. Their healthcare system.

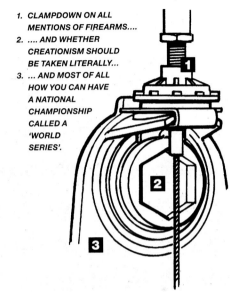

1. *CLAMPDOWN ON ALL MENTIONS OF FIREARMS....*
2. *.... AND WHETHER CREATIONISM SHOULD BE TAKEN LITERALLY...*
3. *... AND MOST OF ALL HOW YOU CAN HAVE A NATIONAL CHAMPIONSHIP CALLED A 'WORLD SERIES'.*

FIG 9•4 **ANGLO-AMERICAN AMITY: KEEPING A TIGHT GRIP ON THE SPECIAL RELATIONSHIP**

A drinking age of 21 and beer only marginally less weak than water. The size of food portions.

These issues remind the British that actually they are much more European in outlook than they are American. As a wise man once said: 'for the American life is always serious and the situation is never hopeless. For the British life is never serious and the situation is always hopeless.'

Basically, the British think the Americans would be greatly improved by being more British.

Model behaviour

1. Apologising

Elton John said that 'sorry seems to be the hardest word'. Not for 65 million of his countrymen it isn't. The British say 'sorry' more than almost any other word, and certainly more than any other nation do. If Neil Armstrong had been British, he wouldn't have said 'one small step for man' as he took his first steps on the moon: instead, he'd have said a breathless litany of apologies for stepping on Buzz Aldrin's toes, for the transmission delay on the pictures, for disturbing the moon's pristine surface, and a hundred other things.

There is almost no situation in which the British will not apologise, whether or not they are at fault. They will apologise if they walk into you or vice versa, even if you are a door or a streetlight. When you pick up the phone to them, they will apologise for disturbing you. They will apologise for being late, being early and being on time. They will apologise for paying with any kind of note which requires the shopkeeper to give more than £5 in change. They will apologise if they mishear you or if you mishear them. They will apologise before you have sex with them, after you've had sex with them, and very probably in the middle of having sex with them too.

2. Reserve

The British don't like to make a scene. No: the British would rather shrivel up and die than make a scene. They would rather catch crippling salmonella from a piece of chicken which is red raw than send it back to the kitchen. Every day in British restaurants, the question 'is everything all right with your meal?' is asked 178,892 times, and not once is the answer anything other than 'yes, lovely, thanks'. For most nations, online booking for restaurants and hotels is a timesaving convenience. For the British it's a lifesaver. They would rather stay at home than have to talk to someone to make a reservation.

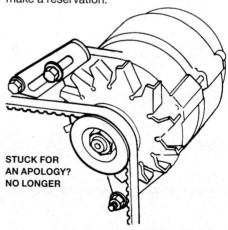

**STUCK FOR
AN APOLOGY?
NO LONGER**

FIG 9•5 **MIND THE GAAAAP
(GREAT AUTOMATIC ALL-PURPOSE
ALL-OCCASION APOLOGY GENERATOR)**

3. Stiff upper lip

The British are masters of stoic understatement. If you ask a Briton 'how are you?' and they reply 'not bad' (which they will), those two words could mean anything from 'I've just won £150m on the lottery' to 'my entire family has been wiped out in a freak meteorite accident'. The proper Brit would regard neither eventuality as cause for overt public emotion.

It's no accident that the British reserve special affection for those who've displayed special stiffness of upper lip, such as:

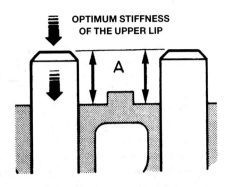

OPTIMUM STIFFNESS OF THE UPPER LIP

FIG 9•6 **MEASURING THE RESISTANCE TO DEFORMATION OF THE SUPERIOR ORAL FOLD**

a) the Antarctic explorer Captain Oates who sacrificed himself to save his companions by leaving with the words 'I may be some time'

b) the Earl of Uxbridge, who at the Battle of Waterloo suffered a serious cannon shot wound and said to the Duke of Wellington: 'by God, Sir, I've lost my leg.' Wellington, who ceded to no one in lip stiffness, looked down and replied 'by God, Sir, so you have.'

c) Lieutenant General Sir Adrian Carton de Wiart, who in the First World War lost an eye, an ear and a hand (including pulling off his own fingers when a doctor declined to amputate), and was also shot in the skull, the ankle, the hip and the leg. 'Frankly,' he said later, 'I enjoyed the war.'

4. Modesty

Carton de Wiart was also awarded the Victoria Cross, the highest award for gallantry in combat, but chose not to mention this in his autobiography. This shows another facet of the Brit, their (usual) unfathomable modesty. It's not just that the British don't like to blow their own trumpet: they don't like people to know that they might even have a trumpet.

Winston Churchill's motto was 'KBO' for 'Keep Buggering On': the KEEP CALM AND CARRY ON meme was originally a British World War Two instruction.

Timing belt

The British are world leaders at waiting in line. They are never happier than when in a public place being funnelled into zig-zag rope barriers. They will queue for anything, anywhere, any time. They will queue on their own. They will queue for important things and unimportant things. They will queue just to be part of a queue, even if that queue is an endless loop or a Möbius strip or some other mathematically challenging concept.

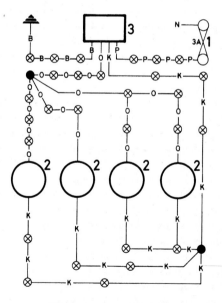

FIG 9•7 **QUEUING SYSTEMS:**
SINGLE CHANNEL, MULTICHANNEL.
SINGLE PHASE, MULTIPHASE

There are clear rules to the British queue, of course

a) Don't cut in. You're in a hurry? Tough. Come back and shop at a time when you're not.

....

b) If someone does try and cut in, tut loudly. Only if this doesn't work can you call them out on it, preferably in as sanctimonious a manner as you can muster. 'Excuse ME! There IS a queue here, you know', followed by an eye-roll and a muttered 'some people' as they take their rightful place behind you.

....

c) The Queuing Collective may choose to let people go ahead under special circumstances (if they're old/disabled/only have one item). But these people must never ask and must start at the back of the queue and only work their way forwards by invitation.

....

d) Examine the contents of other people's baskets or trolleys while you're waiting. Look away quickly when they catch you doing so.

....

e) Don't strike up a conversation with anyone. Where do you think you are? Naples?

f) Check social media, emails or messages on your smartphone.

....

g) Don't get too close to the person in front of you. Maintain an invisible exclusion zone around yourself, confident in the assumption that everyone else will be doing the same thing. Mind the gap.

....

h) At the same time as minding the gap, you must also ensure that the gap is not large enough for someone to sneak in when your attention is distracted (by examining the contents of someone else's basket, for example). This maintenance of a Goldilocks-style space is like finding the biting point on a clutch so you can do a hill start: you will get it wrong once or twice before nailing it.

....

i) If in a situation where two or more queues are in operation, resign yourself to the fact that you will inevitably be in the slowest-moving one. But let everyone else know your dissatisfaction with this state of affairs by tutting (the tut is to the British queuer as the horn is to the Italian driver), looking ostentatiously at your watch and asking in a stage whisper why you always have to get the staff-member-on-training.

Queue confusion

The only way to fox the British when it comes to queuing is to sow doubts in their minds. Take a supermarket where there are manned checkouts one side and self-service ones the other. If there are two distinct queues, then fine: but what about the person who has no preference but is waiting for the first till in either category to become free? He has to hover mid-stream, ready to go either left or right: and soon others will start doing the same, and someone who only wants manned service will find a self-service person cutting in front of them because the self-service is free while at the manned desk Mrs Miggins is still counting out her change, and soon everyone there will know what the Sex Pistols meant when they sang about Anarchy In The UK. At least until the assistant manager comes with an elasticated rope divider.

If you leave the queue for any reason, you can always rejoin. At the back. In the next county or country.

Kit cars

The British do love a bit of tradition, and the more nonsensical or esoteric it appears the better. Judges and barristers wear horsehair wigs, which look absurd and are hideously uncomfortable. Millions listen to the Shipping Forecast on Radio 4 despite having no idea where any of the areas mentioned are and even less inclination to visit them. Millions also listen to the Queen's Speech every Christmas Day, even though she rarely says anything memorable and even if she did, they'd be too drunk to

remember. Morris dancing. The Last Night Of The Proms. There are good reasons for all these things to exist, but most of all they exist just because. Just because they're British.

Eccentric British traditions

Pretty much every weekend in some corner or other of the country, you will find a championship in an event so esoteric that only the British could have thought it up, let alone have gone to the bother of organising anything around it. Here are ten of the best.

NORTH UTSIRE, SOUTH UTSIRE, VIKING, FASTNET, SHANNON, ROCKALL, CROMARTY, FORTH, DOGGER, GERMAN BIGHT AND THE REST. POETRY.

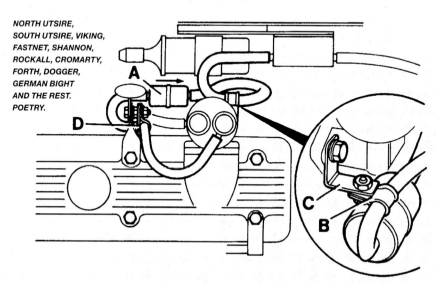

FIG 9•8 **0048, 0052, 1201, 1754: LISTENING TO THE SHIPPING FORECAST**

1. Bog snorkelling

In which the participants navigate through a 60ft peat bog. Allowed: snorkels, masks, flippers. Not allowed: conventional swimming strokes, lifting your head above the bog more than four times. Ideal for those who still think they're seven-year-old boys and/or dogs.

2. Bognor Birdman

In the seaside town of Bognor, would-be Wright brothers run off the end of the pier and try to fly as far as possible in whatever weird and wonderful contraption they've built. For most of them, 'as far as possible' is 'not very far at all'. For all of them, the ultimate destination remains the same: the English Channel.

3. Knob Throwing

The Dorset Knob is a hard biscuit which has a mildly risqué name. An unpromising start for most nations, but not for the British. The annual Knob Festival began as a small event in the village of Cattistock, but has gradually expanded over the years and now attracts thousands to an all-day multi-event show all based on the giggly appeal of the word 'knob'. The blue riband event is the Knob Throwing, and the winner gets to proclaim him or herself 'Dorset's Biggest Tosser'. Makes you proud to be British.

A SCREW, LOOSE

FIG 9•9 **WHAT YOU NEED TO COMPETE IN MOST OF THESE EVENTS**

4. Cheese rolling

Ingredients: 1 steep Gloucestershire hill, 1 18lb wheel of Double Gloucester, several hundred nutters. Roll cheese down hill. Get nutters to follow cheese down hill any way they can. Winner goes home with the cheese and possibly a broken bone or two.

5. Coal carrying

Run for a mile with a sack of coal on your shoulders. Started almost half a century ago with the genesis of most things in Britain – an argument in a pub, on this occasion between two Yorkshire coal merchants as to who was fitter. Also 'in a pub': that idea you had to compete in said race, which seemed like a good idea at a time but quarter of a mile into the actual race probably rather less so.

6. Gurning

Contestants compete to make as ugly an expression as possible. Like a beauty contest but flipped 180 degrees and with no requirement to wear a swimsuit or tell the compère you love working with children and animals.

....

7. Nettle eating

Held in Marshwood, Dorset. Began when a local man – it's always a local man, isn't it? – offered to eat his own 15ft nettle stalk if anyone could beat its size. Whoever can eat most nettle stalks in an hour is the winner (typical amount required to win: 80 feet). Vomiting leads to disqualification.

8. Pooh Sticks

From the game immortalised in Winnie-the-Pooh, when you drop sticks off a bridge into a river and see whose stick reaches a given point first. It is the author's proud and genuine boast that in 2008 he and his daughter were part of 'Sticking To The Prize' which carried off the team gold medal in the world championships: a triumph only slightly tarnished by my mate Paddy losing the silver medal throw-off. To a four-year-old.

....

9. Pram racing

Seven pubs in the town of Oxted, in each of which you have to down a pint. While dressed as a baby. And pushing a 'pram' containing a teammate, who must be a fully grown man. While racing other people doing the same thing. Of course it makes no sense.

....

10. Tar-barrel racing

The West Country is well represented in this tour of madcap japery, and this one is no exception, as it's held in the Devon town of Ottery St Mary. This ranks high on the 'do not try this at home' list (actually, most of them do, come to think of it). Barrels are filled with paper and straw, coated with tar, set aflame and then carried through the streets. Probably something to do with Guy Fawkes or the Spanish Armada. Probably should also lead to all concerned being sectioned.

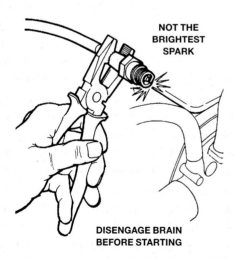

NOT THE BRIGHTEST SPARK

DISENGAGE BRAIN BEFORE STARTING

FIG 9•10 PRE-REQUISITE CONDITIONS FOR TAR-BARREL RACING AND NETTLE EATING

The British sense of humour

The American author Bill Bryson once observed that, if you see two or more British people talking, it is rarely more than a few seconds before one of them makes the other(s) laugh. The British sense of humour is by turns subversive, sardonic, surreal and slapstick, and as often as not involves either the puncturing of pomposity or a refusal to take themselves, or indeed anything, too seriously.

NEVER ASK A CAMPANOLOGIST....

FIG 9•11 ...A QUESTION TO WHICH HE CAN'T REMEMBER THE ANSWER. HE'LL SAY IT DOESN'T RING A BELL

For example

Any time the terrorist threat levels are raised, the old favourite about the Brits having four security levels – Miffed, Peeved, Irritated and A Bit Cross – does the rounds again. Other British threat levels, according to Twitter, include 'would you mind sharing this table?', 'now for a team-building exercise', 'someone you've said goodbye to turns out to be going in the same direction as you', 'running out of ways to say thank you when a stranger holds open three or more doors in a row' and 'I'd Like To Add You To My Professional Network on LinkedIn'.

Almost 400,000 people registered their religion as 'Jedi' in the national census. And of course no general election is complete without representatives not just of the Monster Raving Loony Party but also of the Bus Pass Elvis Party, the Citizens for Undead Rights and Equality, and sundry others dressed as leprechauns, giant strawberries, clowns, druids and the like. Pay your deposit and you're on the ballot paper.

WARNING

When the National Environment Research Council (NERC) asked the public to suggest a name for its new £200m polar research vessel, the runaway winner was 'Boaty McBoatface'. (Moral of the story: name the ship after the managing director's wife, just as always used to be the case.)

Carporting

The British are obsessed with their homes and gardens. You can hardly open a newspaper (if you still open them at all, that is, rather than just call them up on your iPad) or turn on the TV (if you still turn on the TV, that is, rather than just watch on your iPad) without seeing a plethora of property and gardening articles and shows. Where do *Grand Designs* end and *Homes Under The Hammer* begin? Can you *DIY: SOS* without worrying about *Location Location Location*? Have Monty Don and Alan Titchmarsh ever been seen in the same room together? When six or more adults are gathered at the same table, can they go more than 12 minutes without mentioning property prices? These are questions for the greatest philosophers of our age.

Q: How many estate agents does it take to change a light bulb? A: None! The light bulb is in excellent working order. It offers original glass and metal features and is ideally located the middle of the room.

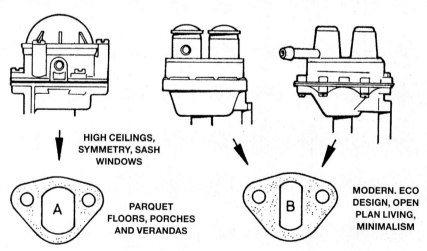

HIGH CEILINGS, SYMMETRY, SASH WINDOWS

PARQUET FLOORS, PORCHES AND VERANDAS

MODERN. ECO DESIGN, OPEN PLAN LIVING, MINIMALISM

FIG 9•12 **THE ENGLISHMAN AND HIS CASTLE: FAVOURITE ARCHITECTURAL STYLES**

⚠ Home obsessed

Why are the British so obsessed with homes and gardens?

There are several reasons. First, there are few rent controls (unlike the Continent), which means the balance of power between landlord and tenant is seen as being overwhelmingly towards the former. Second, the British are very attached to the idea of 'place', especially as they get older and settle down with families: not for nothing is Dunroamin' the clichéd house name. Third, the obsession fuels itself: the more people go on about homes and gardens, the more people will continue to believe they're the be-all and end-all of life.

Political commentators would have you believe World War Three will start in the Middle East or the South China Sea. It won't. It will start midway between numbers 22 and 24 Acacia Avenue in Milton Keynes, where number 22 thinks number 24's conifer blocks out the light, number 24 thinks number 22's leylandii is too tall and an eyesore, and before you know it NATO treaty clauses will be invoked and the world will be aflame. For many Britons, it is less important to have a nice garden than to have a nicer garden than next door's. There are few satisfactions more British than the one gained when seeing one's neighbours at their bedroom window looking down with ill-concealed envy on one's garden.

But most of all, there's the one overarching concern of the British: the reason that the British have to spend so much time indoors and that they can grow almost any variety of plant and flower in their garden. It is, of course, the weather.

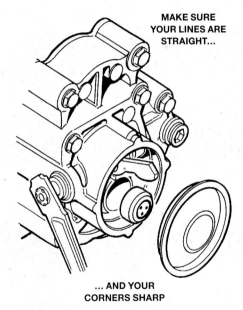

MAKE SURE YOUR LINES ARE STRAIGHT...

... AND YOUR CORNERS SHARP

FIG 9•13 **KEEPING YOUR GARDEN IMMACULATE: INSIDE THE LAWNMOWER**

Driving conditions

'It is commonly observed that when two Englishmen meet their first talk is of the weather.' Dr Johnson.

Every year in Britain it rains. Every year it snows. Every year it suffers a heatwave. And every year the entire nation acts like it's never happened before. The British are very easily pleased this way. If they actually put in place plans to deal with extreme weather ('extreme weather' in Britain meaning 'entirely normal' weather everywhere else), then they'd have nothing to talk about.

Summer

The quickest way to get rid of the sunshine in Britain is to impose a hosepipe ban. If the Met Office talk of a 'barbecue summer', make sure your waterproofs are close at hand. In the Old Testament it rained for 40 days and 40 nights and they called it divine punishment: in Britain they call it summer. When Shakespeare wrote 'shall I compare thee to a summer's day?', he probably didn't mean it as a compliment. If you miss an outdoor concert, don't worry. You can easily recreate the experience by turning the television on, going down to the far end of the garden so you can barely see the screen, and then have someone tip a watering can over your head for three hours.

It's little surprise that the Brits tend to lose their minds on the one or two days a year when the sun does actually come out (before the sun realises it's supposed to be somewhere else, like the Algarve, and buggers off there instead).

IT ONLY RAINS TWICE A WEEK...

... ONCE FOR THREE DAYS AND ONCE FOR FOUR

FIG 9•14 **RAIN GAUGE. OPTIMUM SIZE: LARGE BUCKET – LAKE WINDERMERE**

⚠ The Great British Summer

A Temperature hits 18 degrees Celsius. Italians are still wearing three layers. British remove tops.

Head to pub at 3pm Carve out space in a beer garden which has been empty for the past 364 days but is now standing room only. Start drinking heavily.

Realise that summer has lasted five hours. Wait another 364 days until temperature hits 18 degrees....

FIG 9•15

Don sunglasses to counter glare from everyone else's pasty white legs. Decide to have barbecue.

B Go home. Drag barbecue and charcoal out of storage. Find that barbecue still dirty and charcoal damp. Figure that any germs from barbecue will have died of old age. Go to shop to get new charcoal. Have pushing match with 27 other people who've had the same idea.

Go to supermarket. Buy enough burgers and rolls to feed the 5,000. Go home. Light barbecue. Crack open another tinnie.

Cook the food in the oven instead. Bring food out to garden. Get wet as it begins to rain. Hurry inside.

C Mix enormous jug of Pimm's with fruit and cucumber. That's your five-a-day right there, innit? Discover that flames have gone out.

Check on barbecue after 30 mins. Discover that it hasn't lit. Apply newspaper, firelighters and gasoline to barbecue. Big flames. HUGE flames.

Vehicle classification

If there's one thing the British are even more obsessed with than the weather, their houses and their gardens, it's their class system. At its most basic, the British class system follows the blueprint laid down by John Cleese, Ronnie Barker and Ronnie Corbett in their famous 1966 sketch, in which they stood in order of both height and class.

Cleese: 'I look down on him [Barker] because I am upper-class.'

Barker: 'I look up to him [Cleese] because he is upper-class, but I look down on him [Corbett] because he is lower-class.'

Corbett: 'I know my place.'

Only the British could see someone like Carole Middleton start off as an air hostess, end up as mother-in-law to the future King, and, instead of celebrating such social mobility, sneer at her for having ideas above her station.

Only the British could have invented a show such as _Downton Abbey_, where the upstairs-downstairs divide is spelt out in clear terms.

DO YOU KNOW
THE RULES OF
CROQUET?

DO YOU
LISTEN TO
RADIO 4?

DO YOU
SHOP AT
WAITROSE?

DO YOU KNOW HOW
TO PRONOUNCE
'QUINOA'?

DO YOU PREFER
PIZZA EXPRESS
TO PIZZA HUT?

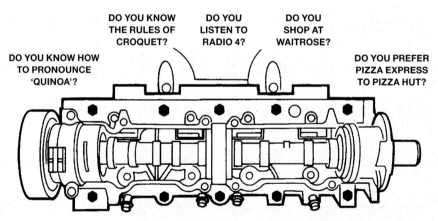

FIG 9•16 **THE MCI² (MECHANISED CONTRAPTION FOR IDENTIFYING MIDDLE-CLASS INDIVIDUALS)**

Of course, the reality is more complex than that

There are divisions within the classes as well as between them. And money is not enough by itself to bridge the gap from one class to another. The upper and upper-middle classes scan the horizon for interlopers like lions on the savannah. Like NSA surveillance operatives looking for terrorist codewords, their antennae are always tuned to the little slip-ups that someone of a different class will make sooner or later. Undercover cops embedded in organised crime gangs don't have to watch their every word as carefully as the social climber does. 'Pardon', 'toilet,' 'serviette', 'settee', 'lounge', 'patio' – to the non-British these are just words, but to the British they are intractable markers of class and breeding.

Proper poshos don't mind turning up at their children's school or at a party in a car so beaten-up it looks as though it's flown through an asteroid belt. They don't mind dressing as though they'd done their entire year's clothes shopping at Oxfam. When it really matters they'll look immaculate, of course, but most of the time their cultivated air of shabbiness is designed to give the impression that they're so secure in their own skin that they don't care what they look like. They believe that pristine clothing and ostentatious displays of wealth are strictly for the nouveaux riche.

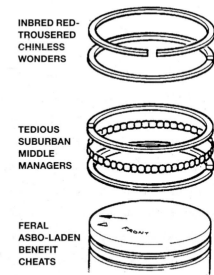

INBRED RED-TROUSERED CHINLESS WONDERS

TEDIOUS SUBURBAN MIDDLE MANAGERS

FERAL ASBO-LADEN BENEFIT CHEATS

FIG 9•17 **EVER-DECREASING CIRCLES: CLASS SYSTEM CLICHÉS**

WARNING

The British obsession with class can permeate even the most unexpected places. Take perhaps Britain's most famous comedy show, Fawlty Towers. 90% of the comedy there stems directly or indirectly from the fact that Basil is (a) a terrible snob (b) terrified of his wife.

Road manners

Britain is a small island with lots of people. It is no surprise that driving can often be fraught and stressful, no matter whether you:

1) have just passed your test and are driving a car whose stereo is worth more than the rest of the vehicle and whose exhaust note could wake the dead

2) are a sales rep in a fleet car with a diesel engine which you thought was efficient and environmentally friendly but have now found out thanks to the government that it is the devil's own work and you are therefore Lucifer's personal chauffeur

3) are driving a 4x4 which is so over-engineered that it could withstand a direct nuclear strike even though you've never taken it any further off-road than the Sainsbury's car park.

4) were born in the 19th century and are therefore driving a mauve Nissan Micra at 22mph on an open road where 60 miles is both the speed limit per hour and the length of the tailback you're causing.

SERIOUS STONE CHIP DAMAGE TO YOUR FRONT BUMPER

SPRINGS MORE KNACKERED THAN THOSE IN JACK NICHOLSON'S BED

FIG 9•18 **THE EFFECT OF BADLY SURFACED BRITISH ROADS ON YOUR CAR**

If you want to go anywhere, make sure you're driving in the small hours and like a vampire are safely at your destination before dawn.

The Haynes Explains Code

The Highway Code lists the official rules of driving on British roads. The HAYNES EXPLAINS Code is here to help you out with the unofficial ones.

a) Don't crawl over speed bumps. They're not land mines. With a decent run-up you can probably get airborne and skim your car between them like a stone on the water.

....

b) When driving in the countryside, acknowledge everyone who lets you through. When driving in the city, acknowledge precisely no one.

....

c) When someone's coming the other way on a single-track road, you must stop, wait for the other person to come forward, and when they fail to do so (because being British they're waiting for you to do so too), reverse at least 2 miles until the road becomes wide enough again.

....

d) Exception to rule c: if the other driver has committed an offence (e.g. gone through a width restrictor when it's not their right of way) then you are entitled to wait until the end of time until they move back.

e) When two lanes become one and someone is trying to sneak in front of you on the outside, go right up close behind the car in front so they can't get in and stare straight ahead so you don't see them mouthing precisely what they think of you.

....

f) Flashing your lights briefly is friendly. Flashing them not-so-briefly indicates your low opinion of the other driver's intelligence and parentage.

....

g) Driving at 40mph on a 60 road will greatly annoy the drivers behind you. Continuing to drive at 40 when you enter a 30 zone and getting flashed by a speed camera will greatly amuse the drivers behind you and make up for some of the annoyance.

....

h) The following phrases are all acceptable when addressed towards your fellow road users:

- 'you could get a bus through there'
- 'get a move on, love, it's not gonna get any greener'
- 'pick a lane: any one will do'
- 'it's the one on the right. Push it down. No, with your foot.'

Fuel

The British run on two types of fuel: tea and beer.

Tea

The British drink 165 million cups of tea per day, or 62 billion cups per year. There is no circumstance in which the British will not drink tea. Literally none. At times of celebration or sadness, in sickness and in health, morning noon and night, whether alone or in a group, someone will within 5 nanoseconds say 'I'll just put the kettle on.'

Making tea involves the perfect amount of fiddling around for the British: enough to ease some of their awkwardness in a social situation without being so much that they risk not being able to perform the task (unlike, for example, assembling an IKEA flat-pack wardrobe).

Tea also offers just about the perfect amount of permutations to be enough for everyone without being unnecessarily confusing.

'Builder's tea'

This is in no way an insult – all British people are equal before the mighty tealeaf – but at its most genuine must be drunk with plenty of milk and enough sugar to allow the spoon to stand up straight of its own accord.

'Posh tea'

Also known as Earl Grey, named after the 26th Prime Minister. Charles Grey helped abolish slavery and have the seismic 1832 Reform Act passed, but it is as tea that he is best known, and there is no higher honour for a British person than that.

'Herbal tea'

This is not really proper tea but it comes in nice colourful packets and offering it to people after dinner is a diplomatic way of saying 'right, drink this and then bugger off, I want to go to bed.' If they plump for coffee and/ or a nightcap, they'll be there till the small hours.

ADD BOILING WATER TO TEA BAG IN MUG AND LEAVE FOR TWO MINUTES

MAX
MIN

REMOVE BAG, ADD MILK, LEAVE FOR SIX MINUTES. THEN DRINK

FIG 9•19 **MAKING THE PERFECT CUP OF TEA**

Beer

If a Briton ever invites you for a 'swift half' after work, be prepared to wake up at midday the next day in someone else's clothes, in the middle of a roundabout 55 miles from where you started, with a pneumatic drill hammering away inside your head and with only the vaguest memory of what happened the night before. (If, on the other hand, you make plans for a 'massive session', you can be sure you'll be tucked up in bed by 10.30 with *Newsnight*, a cup of Ovaltine and a vague sense that the evening wasn't all it was cracked up to be.)

The British love beer. Bitter is often brewed locally and therefore comes in all strengths and with suitably esoteric names to boot. British men in particular can think of no more enjoyable way to pass an evening than by drinking anywhere between half a dozen and a dozen pints, leading each other in lusty but tuneless renditions of tasteless drinking songs, before repairing to either a curry house or a kebab shop (all the best British foods are ethnic) and wending their way home in the small hours.

Saying 'beer can' in an English accent and 'bacon' in a Jamaican accent sound exactly the same.

Coffee shops

It's true that the nation's high streets are littered with coffee shops belonging to chains with suspiciously foreign names. The true Briton is happy to patronise such establishments yet remains ancestrally suspicious of them, not because he suspects some of them of not paying their taxes (corporate tax avoidance is high on the list of 'things the Brits grumble about but make no real effort to change') but because they don't understand tea. Not really. Not properly. And that's why you'll never hear the British ever referring to coffee towels, coffee dances, storms in coffee cups or 'more coffee, vicar?'

THAT BIT WHICH HISSES A LOT

THAT BIT WHICH GURGLES A LOT

FIG 9•20 **THOSE SHINY MACHINES THEY USE IN FANCY COFFEE SHOPS**

Model history

2500 BC

After scouring the country for a suitable site, ancient Britons decide to build Stonehenge just next to the A303 on the grounds that people stuck in Bank Holiday traffic would welcome the distraction. The stone circle design beats off five other proposals:

1) Bonehenge, made entirely of bones
2) Clonehenge, made of identical copies of Dolly the Sheep
3) Cronehenge, made from old ladies dressed in black
4) Dronehenge, hovering 500 feet above the landscape
5) Sconehenge, made of small lightly sweetened cakes with added fruit.

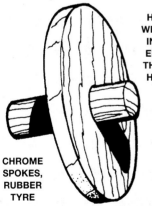

HANG ON. WE HAVEN'T INVENTED EITHER OF THOSE YET, HAVE WE?

CHROME SPOKES, RUBBER TYRE

FIG 9•21 **ITEM 237, HALFORDS CATALOGUE, 78 BC. 'YE WHEELE'**

AD 878

King Alfred burns the cakes while thinking about how to rescue Britain from the Vikings. This gives him the idea for the Great Mercian Bake Off, but the BBC reject the format and tell him it has no audience appeal. Alfred declares war on all commissioning editors.

1027

King Cnut sets his throne on the seashore and commands the incoming tide not to get him wet. The tide is having none of it and soaks him. This incident gives rise to the well-known Anglo-Saxon phrase 'you really are a stupid Cnut'.

1066

The Normans invade. Unable to beat them militarily, the English choose to do so by the national method of taking the piss: in this case, by appropriating the name 'Norman' as an archetypal name for the greyest and most boring of suburban men.

1215

King John signs the Magna Carta. Not to be confused with any or all of the following: Hawaiian private investigator Magnum, P.I., 39th US President Jimmy Carter, or indie band Carter The Unstoppable Sex Machine.

1532-1547

All women named Anne, Catherine and Jane make themselves scarce in case Henry VIII decides he wants to marry them.

1649

Charles II is beheaded and Oliver Cromwell becomes Lord Protector. He bans pubs, theatres, sports, and allows walking on Sunday only to and from church. After 11 years of Funtime Ollie, the British decide they'd rather go back to the system of inbred corrupt monarchy which had worked well for the previous 600 years.

1815-1914

Britain establishes the largest empire in world history by sending young men in thick woollen suits to the hottest parts of the world and ordering them to subdue the natives before they expire of heat exhaustion. Charles Napier celebrates conquering the Indian province of Sindh by sending the one-word telegram 'Peccavi', Latin for 'I have sinned.' Napier is forevermore thought of as the most insufferable smartarse.

1939-45

Winston Churchill single-handedly wins (a) One-Liner of the Year award seven years running (b) World War Two.

2016-17

Stung by criticism that politics is 'boring' and 'for squares', the Conservative Party decide to liven things up and enact their own *Game of Thrones* spin-off by:

a) having a referendum which is more divisive than anything since the Civil War of 1642-51
b) stabbing each other in the back and occasionally the front in the search for a new leader
c) calling another election in case no one had had quite enough of it all
d) not really losing that election but not really winning it either and no one knows what's going on so we'll probably be having another one soon. In fact we might as well enclose a ballot paper with every copy of this book just to save the Electoral Commission some cash.

2018

At time of print in 2017, after the historic few years in politics, it's anyone's guess...

Recreational vehicle

The British are a sports-mad nation, though often with more enthusiasm than skill. They are increasingly good at winning Olympic gold medals, usually in sports which involve sitting down such as rowing, sailing and cycling. (Talking of cycling, four out of the past five Tours de France at the time of writing had been won by

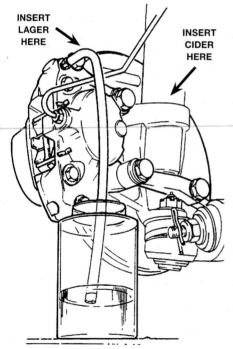

INSERT
LAGER
HERE

INSERT
CIDER
HERE

Britons, albeit ones born in Belgium and Kenya respectively.)

Having invented football, the British are now increasingly bad at it – well, not so much Wales, who reached the semi-finals of Euro 2016, but certainly England, who in the same tournament contrived to lose to Iceland (a nation with a population roughly 1/200th the size), and Scotland, who didn't even qualify and have in the past managed to lose to the Faeroe Islands (population: lots of puffins and a bloke who sells bobble hats).

Cricket

Luckily the English still have cricket, which asides from its other merits has the added benefit of being totally incomprehensible to Americans:

a) The batsmen are in when they're out in the field and out when they're back in the pavilion
b) A tie and a draw are different things
c) The terminology is so arcane that even Hunter S. Thompson on an epic drugs binge couldn't have made it up. Chin music, corridor of uncertainty, cow corner, googly, Mankadding, nightwatchman, silly mid-off, wagon wheel, yorker, zooter. These are all real terms.

Famous moments in British sport

Year	Sport	Result	Notes
1877	Cricket	England lose to Australia	A set of bails are burned and put in a miniature urn. Thus the Ashes is born, and with it a never-ending struggle between whingeing Poms and convicts.
1966	Football	England win the World Cup	And never stop going on about it afterwards. A Russian linesman gives a goal that probably wasn't. Jack Charlton wakes up the next morning on a stranger's sofa in Leytonstone.
1981	Cricket	England win the Ashes	To be more precise, Ian Botham wins the Ashes, and thus gives the BBC something to shove on during any rain break for years to come. At least until Sky buys all the rights, that is.
1990	Football	England reach the World Cup semi-final	And lose to Germany. On penalties. Chris Waddle's kick has now reached Saturn and will soon go interstellar. Germany enjoy the experience so much that they do exactly the same to England six years later in Euro 96.
1992	Cricket	England reach the World Cup final.	And lose to Pakistan. They had previously reached the final in 1979 against the West Indies. And lost. And in 1987 against Australia. And lost.
2003	Rugby	England win the World Cup	Jonny Wilkinson drops the winning goal with 30 seconds to go and smiles shyly. Rumour has it that Martin Johnson may also have smiled. Once. No photographic evidence of the latter exists.
2012	Olympics	Team GB come third in the medal table	London astonishes itself and everyone else by putting on a brilliant Games after moaning about the cost/waste/weather/disruption for the previous seven years.
2013	Tennis	Andy Murray wins Wimbledon	Andy Murray becomes national hero. 54 million English people insist he's 'British' having previously insisted he was 'Scottish'.
2016	Football	England lose 2-1 to Iceland	National humiliation. Also: why the hell are the national team playing against a supermarket? Imagine what the score would have been if they'd got in a few ringers from Aldi and Lidl too.

In-car entertainment

Britain is a nation of writers, and none more so than William Shakespeare, he who could never buy a drink for love or money. (Shakespeare walks into a pub. The landlord says 'Get out! You're Bard.') Shakespeare's famous the world over, though Haynes Explains can't quite understand why: his comedies aren't funny (you want funny? Peter Kay, he's funny) and his idea of a love story is one where one teenager seduces another and then everyone dies. Besides, he doesn't know what he's on about half the time. 'All the world's a stage'? Incorrect. All the world is the third planet from the Sun, formed around 4.5 billion years ago and divided into several rigid tectonic plates which migrate across the surface over periods of many millions of years. Sorry to be pedantic, Billy boy, but this is basic stuff.

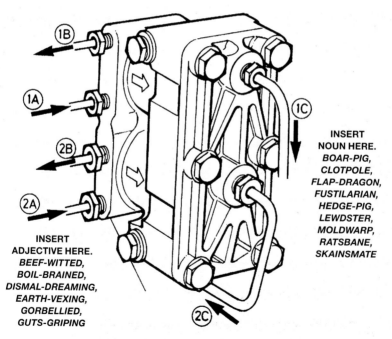

INSERT NOUN HERE.
*BOAR-PIG,
CLOTPOLE,
FLAP-DRAGON,
FUSTILARIAN,
HEDGE-PIG,
LEWDSTER,
MOLDWARP,
RATSBANE,
SKAINSMATE*

INSERT ADJECTIVE HERE.
*BEEF-WITTED,
BOIL-BRAINED,
DISMAL-DREAMING,
EARTH-VEXING,
GORBELLIED,
GUTS-GRIPING*

FIG 9•23 **RANDOM SHAKESPEARE INSULT GENERATOR**

⚠ Other famous writers

Jane Austen

Who can barely let a page go by without someone drawing attention to an inadequate dowry, riding off on the nearest available horse in a huff, losing face, finding face again, or all the above.

Charles Dickens

Who after an indecisive start ('It was the best of times, it was the worst of times': come on, Chuck, get off the fence and tell us which one it was) got into his stride with some of the best names ever invented (Wackford Squeers, Dick Swiveller, Charity Pecksniff, Woolwich Bagnet and Pleasant Riderhood among others). Also famous for the fact that on the old £10 note, if you combined his hair with the Queen's face you got John McEnroe.

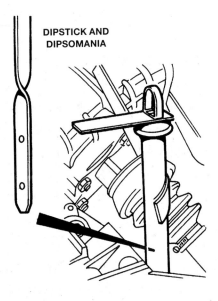

DIPSTICK AND
DIPSOMANIA

FIG 9•24 **THE GREATEST NOVEL JANE AUSTEN NEVER WROTE**

Geoffrey Chaucer

Bawdy medieval poet. If he was around today he would surely be a rapper, perhaps easing Eric B out of the picture to form Geoffrey C & Rakim: 'So Ich start mye myssyon/ Leave mye resydence/ Thynkynge how coulde Ich get summe dead presydentes/ Ich neede moneye/ Ich used to be a stykke-uppe kydde/ So Ich thynke of all ye devyouse thynges Ich did.'

George Orwell

Named after the river. Wanted to call himself 'George Mississippi' but publishers said it wouldn't fit on the cover. Most famous for Nineteen Eighty-Four, which has entered the culture in many different ways, most notably an affable Geordie saying 'day 44 in the Big Brother household' and Frank Skinner discussing pet hates with various celebrities on *Room 101*.

Fault diagnosis

Fault	Diagnosis	Treatment
Feel sick.	You had a skinful last night.	Let's have a nice cup of tea. I'll put the kettle on.
Feel exhausted.	You had a rough day at work failing to tell boss exactly what you think of him.	Let's have a nice cup of tea. I'll put the kettle on.
Can't stop apologising.	You're British. It's in your DNA.	Let's have a nice cup of tea. I'll put the kettle on.
Can't keep any food down.	You have campylobacter and salmonella because you didn't want to make a scene in the restaurant by sending back food you knew was undercooked.	Let's have a nice cup of tea. I'll put the kettle on.
Feet hurt.	You've been standing in a queue for three hours.	Let's have a nice cup of tea. I'll put the kettle on.
Green with envy.	You've spent the entire weekend surfing for property porn. Stop looking at houses you'll never be able to afford on primelocation.com.	Let's have a nice cup of tea. I'll put the kettle on.
Stiff back.	You've been sitting in a car for five hours. Yes, I know you only went 20 miles. You want no traffic jams, go live in the Mojave desert.	Let's have a nice cup of tea. I'll put the kettle on.
Feel shaken.	Someone tried to talk to me on the Tube today.	Let's have a nice cup of tea. I'll put the kettle on.
Feel sad.	The England football team lost. To Vanuatu.	Let's have a nice cup of tea. I'll put the kettle on.
Feel happy.	The England football team lost. To Vanuatu. But am Scottish.	Let's get hammered. I'll crack open the whisky.

Conclusion

The British can at first appear a rum bunch, full of contradictions.

For example, their detective programmes are set in the most genteel locations – the kind of places where in real life a Mars bar falling from a newsagent's shelf is news – and yet involve the kind of murder rates which would shame South Central LA, Cuidad Juarez and Helmand Province. How and why there are still people living in places like Midsomer, let alone people voluntarily visiting, is a mystery. Not to mention the fact that all those murders must be playing merry havoc with the property prices.

Secondly, what they say is not what they mean. A Brit who tells you something 'is not bad' thinks it's the best thing ever. 'I hear what you say' means 'You're wrong'. 'It's my fault' means 'it's your fault'. 'Interesting' means either 'boring' or 'insane' depending on the context. 'You must come to dinner soon' means 'you must come to dinner never, absolutely never'. It takes a while to get used to this way of speaking, but eventually it will become second nature and you will be able to decode the Brit as easily as you've adapted to driving on the left, the *left*! FOR GOD'S SAKE KEEP LEFT WHAT ARE YOU DOING YOU LUNATIC?

Third, they tune in to the worst kind of musical talent shows, where people who can't sing are tempted by the prospect of a contract which will make them no money and a career which will last roughly as long as a British summer. Yet this is the nation which produced the Beatles and the Stones, Led Zep and Pink Floyd, Blur and Oasis and any number of other musicians for the ages.

In fact, scrap the 'can at first appear'. No 'appear' about it. They are a rum bunch all right. But a pretty good bunch too, on the whole. They're a people of a million small kindnesses, of generous spirit and tolerance, and of a healthy disregard for taking things too seriously. Yes, they're a good bunch all right.

Even the Scots.

Sometimes.

Perhaps the most British tweet ever was one which accompanied a picture of Prince Harry. He was on duty in Afghanistan, wearing camouflage uniform and a hi-vis tabard. 'Make up your mind, mate,' someone had tweeted. 'Do you want to be seen or not?'

Titles in the Haynes Explains series

Now that Haynes has explained The British, you can progress to our full size manuals on car maintenance (to safely travel the green and pleasant land), *Caravan Manual* (glamping on wheels), *Cricket Manual* (just is rather than just not) and *Men's Baking Manual* (for the Great British variety).

There are Haynes manuals on just about everything – but let us know if we've missed one.

Haynes.com